Sullivan Strong

Sullivan Strong

Lessons in the School of Hard Knocks

MIKE SULLIVAN

gatekeeper press™

Columbus, Ohio

Sullivan Strong: Lessons in the School of Hard Knocks

Published by Gatekeeper Press
2167 Stringtown Rd, Suite 109
Columbus, OH 43123-2989
www.GatekeeperPress.com

ISBN (paperback): 9781662907029

Dedicated to my wife Dana, our children, and our grandchildren pictured above. From left to right: Ryan, Emma, Hunter, Sarah, Michael, Ava, Ayden, and Kate.

Life is hard. You get knocked around a lot. It is difficult to pick the winners from the losers. Some stay on top of their game most of their lives, while others struggle and never seem to get ahead in the game. We all share the same fate: death. If we are lucky, people will remember a picture of us on a wall. "Hey, that's Papa Mike. He was a Marine I think."

We all suffer, and everyone has a cross or two to bear in this life. Some carry their crosses better than others, but we all get wounded. There are no exceptions. Another truth is that death is not a team sport. In life, we come in alone and we go out alone. None of us knows when the stopwatch will signal, "Time's up."

Most of us are not consumed by the thought of our own death. If we were, we wouldn't get out of bed in the morning. We go about our day taking care of business. We stumble, we fall, and we get back in the game. We either accept responsibility for our failures, or blame someone else. Either way, we suffer.

I've been lucky to have lived a life filled with love and joy. I have two loving children, a wife who has stayed with me almost fifty years, and eight beautiful grandchildren. I was raised by two parents who loved me and a brother who is still my best friend. My kids all married wonderful spouses who Dana and I love dearly. Bryan, Katy, and Jennie supported my children and our family through thick and thin. I had the opportunity to make a career in the United States Marine Corps and to teach high school students. Most importantly, I received the gift of faith from my parents, Mary and John Sullivan.

I have also experienced great sorrow and despair. I have held my mother's hand as she passed from this world and watched the pain in my father's eyes as he succumbed to lung cancer. I have told two of my grandchildren that their father was not coming home. I have been addicted to alcohol and had personal setbacks that have pushed me to the edge. I have surveyed the world without Mike Sullivan. In short, I too have been wounded.

We all have our roles to play in life; mother, father, brother, leader, follower, friend, or teacher. The list is endless. We all have different vocations and unique life experiences. The road in life is filled with potholes and curves, as well as open straightaways. Sometimes you have to slow down and take in the scenery to appreciate your surroundings. At other times, when the road is clear, you can speed up.

Despite the road conditions, we all have to follow the rules of the road. We have to drive defensively to avoid those potholes. It is the same in life. We need a set of beliefs and core values to get us through the tough times, especially when we cannot see the road ahead. Without stop signs, green lights, and caution signals, it is likely we will crash and do great harm to ourselves and others.

I am writing this short book to capture what I believe to be my life's greatest lessons. Not unlike the rules posted on the road, these "life" rules have guided me through some very challenging times.

Like you, I have read my share of self-help books that promise to make life more manageable and more fulfilling. But the truth is that the best learning takes place in the school of hard knocks. Smart people learn from their mistakes, while others never move forward after stumbling down. Life is not complicated, although many of us make it so. We fail to listen to our inner voice that tells us to slow down, think about what we are doing, and change direction if we are headed down a one-way street.

It often feels like time is racing and getting away from us. Our wisdom crawls along and is acquired over time, usually after we make a wrong turn in the road. My hope is that by writing this book I will help others stay focused on the road of life and avoid potholes. I hope my grandchildren will read this book. My prayer is that all of them will be honorable men and women who adhere to the simple rules I have laid out in this book.

Rule 1: Family is Forever

Your best friends in life will most likely be your fellow family members. No matter how many times you fall, they will be there to pick you up. It may be a brother or a sister who you can always count on. Cherish the relationships you have with all your uncles, aunts, and cousins. Never let a day go by without thanking your mom and dad for the gifts they have given you, especially the gift of life. Knowing your family's history helps define your own character and gives you a sense of pride and respect for those who have traveled the road of life ahead of you.

From a very young age, I always tried to make my parents proud of me. Dad always talked about his own dad, my grandfather John, who quit school in 1911 to go to work in a shoe factory. His father left his wife and five kids for alcohol and the company of another woman. Being an Irish Catholic, my great grandmother could not divorce her husband. My grandfather had to pick up the slack and go to work making thirty cents an hour sweeping floors in a shoe factory. Eventually, he worked himself up the ladder of success and became the shop foreman.

I met my grandfather only twice in my life. He was a widower. My grandmother, Annie, died in her early fifties from a stroke. Her father was a First Sergeant in the 24th Maine

Volunteers and fought at the Battle of Gettysburg. She went to Mass every day and made sure my dad became an altar boy. Her last moments on this earth were spent clutching her rosary saying a Hail Mary.

What I do remember about Grandpa John Patrick Sullivan was his kindness and ability to tell a story. He loved talking about my father and his sister, Aunt Esther. He was very calm and quiet most of the time. When he talked about his upbringing, he always mentioned how much he loved his mother and his siblings. He never mentioned his father who had abandoned his family, or the dreary eleven-hour days he spent in the Frye Boot factory. Rather, he talked about the value of hard work and sacrifice. He always said, "Any job worth doing is worth doing to the best of your abilities." He was grateful for his life and his family.

Grandpa Sullivan was Irish through and through. He took great pride in his heritage and always sent us a funny card on Saint Patrick's Day. Unlike his father, he was a moderate drinker. The only time I heard him mention his father was in connection to what he called the "Irish Curse."

My father was a Navy fighter pilot who had flown combat missions in World War II and the Korean War. He was disciplined and methodical. He laid out his goals, stayed focused, and was self-reliant. But he also had great compassion for people who needed help. He never missed an opportunity to remind us kids how lucky we were. He had been raised during the Great Depression and knew first-hand how rough life could be without material comforts.

My mother's parents were Grace and William Stiles. William Stiles was a World War I Army captain who fought in the trenches of France. He was decorated for single-handedly charging a German machine gun nest and saving the lives of his fellow soldiers. Before I was born, he died from a stroke while rocking in a chair on his front porch. My Grandma Grace made sure I knew all about his bravery and his loyal, upright character. She always reminded me how lucky I was to be a descendant of a true hero. When I look at the pictures of my parents and grandparents, I feel great respect and pride. They were honorable people who made great sacrifices for their children and our nation.

I met my wife, Dana, fifty years ago. Once a shy girl, she is now the director of a regional office. She possesses the inner strength to persevere through the toughest of times, including the loss of our son John. She is a person of action. She is compassionate and kind, but she can also be demanding and disciplined. It must be that German blood—her maiden name was Rudershausen. She too was blessed with parents who loved her and provided her with great role models. We both loved our parents and tried to live up to their expectations. We tried to make them proud of us.

We are all products of our upbringing and environment. If we are strong, disciplined, compassionate, and understanding, chances are we inherited those qualities from our parents. If we are filled with doubt, anxiety, selfishness, and maybe even cruel behaviors, it could be we learned these traits growing up. If we see we are on the wrong road, we can all back up and go the other way. But it sure does help if we have learned the value of faith, hope, friendship, commitment, and uprightness while growing up in a loving home.

When we have kids, we assume immense responsibilities. Our kids become our "immortal masterpieces." I heard this term from a Catholic priest while he baptized my son, John, back in 1976. It's true. It is from the family we receive the strength to stand up against the winds that seek to blow us off course in life. We have done our job if we give our kids the inner strength to stand up for what is right and just, to have faith that things can get better, to be positive in their approach to challenges, and to always help those in need. In short, we want our kids to be comfortable in their own skin and possess the confidence to succeed in life. We cannot accomplish this task without setting the example through our own behaviors.

Perhaps most importantly, we want to build strong emotional connections with our kids. When they get into trouble, we want them to ask us for help. These emotional connections cannot be overemphasized. When kids suffer, parents suffer. When kids isolate and try to take on the burdens of life alone, it can lead to great pain and even tragedy.

Our family is our safe haven. It is where we first learn the difference between right and wrong, develop our value system, and gain the confidence to get on the field to compete in the game of life. Our parents are there to pick us up when we fail and to give us a pat on the back when we do succeed. Friends go, but family lasts forever. We should continually seek ways to strengthen the family bonds that keep us together. Never take your family for granted.

Rule 2: Have Patience

My mother and father both taught me patience. Mom was a good listener and Dad cracked the whip if you got out of line. Before he spanked me as a child he always said, "*This is going to hurt me more than you, Michael.*" He never hit you hard, but it was firm. I could always count on both of them for emotional support and to provide me the guidance I needed to navigate around some deep potholes along the rough road of life.

When I was five, I had to learn to tie my shoes. To get into kindergarten at Sacred Heart Catholic School, students needed to be able to tie their own shoes. I tried really hard, but I just could not tie the right knot. Mom spent hours with me and one day I finally got it. I learned to tie my shoes!

Mom told me that if I really worked hard at anything in life, I could succeed. She always said, "*Remember, Michael, patience is a virtue. Good things come to those who wait.*" Mom did not let me give up. She built up my confidence and made me feel successful. As a parent and even as a grandparent, you are first and foremost a teacher. Kids learn from your actions and the way you handle the ups and downs in life. My mom and dad were not perfect, but I always knew they loved us. They were both patient people.

When I was young, I had a hard time being patient. I wanted things my way, and right now. I envisioned where I wanted to go and learned to work hard to achieve my goals. Most of the time I like to think I knew where I was going, but like everyone else, I experienced my own self-doubts. I took wrong turns on the road throughout my teenage years.

In the Marine Corps, I pushed my Marines very hard. I always had time to talk to each one of them about their personal lives. Knowing your troops and looking out for their welfare is one of the leadership principles they teach young Marine officers. I realized that without patience and understanding, I could not successfully lead my unit. Every one of us has strengths and weaknesses. As individuals, we often fail. But as a team, we can often exceed our expectations. The key to being a successful leader is to tap into those individual strengths and to work on the weaknesses to ensure the team is successful. Without patience, you will fail.

When I first took over my thirty-man platoon, another Marine came up to me and said, "Good luck with these under-achievers." I was shocked that any senior officer would refer to Marines in this manner. Every Marine I ever worked with needed a little polishing. They were all capable men and women who, in my humble opinion, just needed a little rudder and encouragement. After one month of working with my young lads, I discovered half of them could not read. It was the 1970s during the post-Vietnam era when you did not need a high school diploma to enter into military service. My men could not even read their equipment's technical manuals.

There was a new program starting on base called the "Reading Advancement Program." We enrolled all our Marines in the program and within a couple of months, we started seeing results; more promotions, better inspection results, and an increase in morale. Simple solutions to complex problems often work. Teach a man or woman to read and you open up the world for them.

Being a good platoon leader required patience and total commitment. Like me, many times my men could not, so to speak, "tie their shoes." No matter what the obstacles ahead, I had to work with them and get them to believe they could accomplish the mission. *Success breeds success.* Once they gained their confidence and started depending on each other, success came.

Any success I had as a Marine is directly related to my upbringing and the patience I was taught under my parents' love and guidance. It is that simple. Raising children requires extraordinary patience. You have to view your kids as works in progress. You cannot judge them on any single event, like a poor report card or getting into trouble with the neighborhood kids. You have to give them the latitude to learn from their mistakes, but always let them know you are there for them. If you're lucky, they will model your good behaviors and develop a solid value system that will get them through the tough times in life.

Kids will struggle with their self-image, especially during their teenage years. Through all their ups and downs, you need to exercise patience. Without patience, and keeping in mind they are your immortal masterpieces, you will be disappointed and may even give up on them. If you tell them they can do something, you will give them the confidence to succeed. If you tell them they are losers, they will live up to that expectation.

Anything in life worth the effort requires hard work and patience. Sports teaches you the art of being patient. You wait for the right pitch in baseball, you take the next wave because this one is closing out, or you hold off on throwing the deep pass. Patience is waiting for the right time to take advantage of your opponent to win the game.

When I was seven, Dad took me to a baseball field to hit fly balls. He taught me how to catch a baseball and I got pretty good at it. My dad was very patient with me. I would often miss the fly ball, or misjudge the depth of the ball coming at me from above. He just kept hitting that ball to me for at least an hour every day. He was a firm believer that "practice makes perfect."

When I turned nine, Dad signed me up for Little League. I played on teams all through high school and Dad watched most of my games. He sat on the benches and was quiet. After the game, he would tell me how good I did. He never criticized me, even if I struck out or missed a fly ball. He was my strongest fan.

In 7th grade, we moved from Imperial Beach to Lafayette, California. I was playing Pony League for a local team. I needed a new baseball glove, but the glove I had my eye on was about $25.00. I knew we could not afford it. One day, my dad took me into the sporting goods store and asked me to show him the glove I wanted. He bought me that glove. It was like hitting a home run! I got a super glove, which I used for the next five years. I made a lot of catches with that glove.

I am sure my dad and mom had to make some financial sacrifices in order to get me that glove. Parents do without so that their kids can have what they need. I had great parents who showed all of us kids the true meaning of love and family. Most importantly, my dad and mom never gave up on me.

A lot of people just want to give up early on themselves, their family, other people, and life in general. They have no staying power. They want quick fixes and instant results. This is a pandemic with many young people today. When they don't get what they want or expect, they switch channels or move to another Facebook page. Personal sacrifice is a concept they just don't get. They have never really had to give up anything to get what they often take for granted: financial security, health, a loving mom and dad. They have no skin in the game and no one has taught them patience. Sad.

We are all "works in progress." Accepting the fact that there is no perfection in the world is the key to developing patience. Sometimes what we expect from others does not measure up to our expectations. There is an old saying my father used a lot. It went something like this, *"When I was fourteen, my father was ignorant. When I turned twenty-one, I was amazed at how much he had learned in seven years."* You see the world from where you sit. We need to exercise patience with everyone if we are going to give them a chance to grow and learn.

Rule 3: Every Day is Your Qualification Day

In the Marines, you have to qualify every year on the rifle range. It is a big thing to win a shooting badge. You strive to achieve an expert badge, but you will settle for a marksman badge. You don't want to go "unqualified."

Your qualification day comes after two weeks of preparation. You fire your weapon from distances as far as five hundred yards. On "qual" day, you pray for no wind, a keen eye, and the patience to hold back on the trigger and gently squeeze off your shots. After ninety minutes of firing fifty rounds, you receive your score. You either get a scowl from your Drill Instructor, or a congratulatory smile. The stakes are high on the rifle range on your qual day. For the next year, you either wear a shooting badge on your uniform, or not. The rifle range teaches Marines to have patience, to have confidence, and to focus. Without these three elements working in harmony, you will not qualify with your rifle.

Like the rifle range, there are no do-overs in life. You qualify once a year; you live each day once. I have tried to live my life as if every day was a qualification day.

Each day we wake up is a blessing. We have the opportunity to help others and can reach out to those who have stumbled and fallen. We should truly appreciate the gifts we have been given. Yesterday is important, but not as important as today. For sure, we should reflect on our past and take pride in our accomplishments. But, too much "self-praise" can lead to your becoming complacent and satisfied with mediocrity. I guess another way of putting it is, "don't rest on your laurels." Don't become the "would've, could've, should've" type of individual who just rests on their past accomplishments. These people are stuck in neutral and not moving forward.

A Marine general once said to me, *"Mike, if we are on the field and not moving the ball forward, we are failing as leaders."* Each day, we need to move forward and improve ourselves; mentally, physically, and spiritually. Making a mistake is not the problem. The problem is getting stuck in neutral and not moving in a positive direction.

History is filled with stories of men and women who performed magnificently well on their "qualification day." This nation's greatest leaders were all tested in life. Each of us will have our own defining moments in our own lives. When I taught high school, I always liked to talk about Joshua Chamberlain, a very famous Civil War hero who fought for the Union forces. His defining moment came on the 3rd of July in 1863.

Before the war, he was a college professor at Bowdoin College in Maine. He was a man filled with humility. His fellow faculty members remembered him as a man of great principle who spoke softly. He taught ethics and poetry.

When the war broke out, he felt it was his duty to fight against the Confederacy and against the institution of slavery. He left behind his wife and children and joined the 20th Maine Volunteers.

He led his unit during the greatest battle of the war, Gettysburg. Today, he is known as the Hero of Little Round Top. If he and his 20th Maine volunteers had not held Little Round Top, the battle of Gettysburg might have been won by the Confederacy. The entire course of American history may have been rewritten without this man's personal courage and leadership to inspire his men to hold (stay in place) the left flank of the Union Army. When his regiment ran out of ammo, he ordered his soldiers to "fix bayonets." He then ordered his men to charge downhill and attack the North Carolinians, an action that saved the day and avoided a Union disaster.

Colonel Chamberlain was later promoted to General, wounded twice more during the war, and was at Appomattox when General Lee surrendered to General Grant. General Grant selected General Chamberlain to help accept the surrender of the Confederate forces. As the soldiers passed by his position, they laid down their arms. Joshua Chamberlain was deeply respected by both sides of the war for the courage and leadership he displayed during every battle. After the war, he was elected the Governor of Maine four times, and later became the President of Bowdoin College. He died at age eighty-four from an infection. The infection was caused by a bullet fragment that remained lodged in his body for over forty years.

Joshua Chamberlain is symbolic to me of the millions of people who go about their day doing the best they can in all the struggles that life throws their way. Very few of us have experienced the challenge that Joshua Chamberlain experienced that day on Little Round Top. We all have personal hurdles to get over in life. Every time we make it over that obstacle, we get stronger.

We are all role models to our family members, co-workers, employees, maybe even students. My dad always said, "One bad decision can wipe out all the good ones you have made." That is why we need to be strong and upright when our defining moments come in life. Just like the rifle range and winning a shooting badge, you have to wear your character for the rest of your life.

There is another quote I like from the great Olympic runner, Jesse Owens. His qual day came in the 1936 Olympic Games held in Berlin. Adolph Hitler was in the stands as Jesse, the only African American athlete on the field, beat all the competition in the one-hundred-yard dash. The crowd went silent. How could what the Nazi Party considered an inferior human being beat the Aryan (white) men on the field? When he returned to the United States, a newsman asked Jesse to comment on the strategy he used to beat the competition. Jesse replied, *"Don't look back. Someone is gaining on you."* Sage advice.

Colonel Rich Higgins, deceased, was an inspiration to me. On the morning of February 1988, Rich and I drove in from Israel and crossed the border into Lebanon. After the morning meeting at our headquarters, we crossed paths in the parking lot. I was heading up to my observation post and Rich was going to the city of Tyre for a meeting with a local leader. As the Commanding Officer of Observer Group Lebanon, he represented the United Nations in all negotiations with the warring factions in southern Lebanon.

"Mike, watch our convoy close today. I have the meeting at ten and should be coming back about 1300 (1 pm) or so." More than his words, I remember the look in his eyes. He seemed unusually concerned. He was a very intuitive man and I believe he sensed the danger, maybe even the end. *Courage is acting in the face of fear.* During his return from the meeting, Rich was kidnapped. He was later tortured by Hezbollah terrorists and murdered.

Rich rests peacefully in Quantico National Cemetery. He was in all respects the finest officer I ever served with in the Marines. I visit him each time I travel to Virginia. Rich's favorite line was, *"One man or woman can make a difference in our world."* The kindness, encouragement, and personal support we show others makes a difference. The simplest things we do to model good and upright character is the way in which we have a positive impact on others. That is how each of us makes the world a better place to live in.

We often get steamrolled in life. We are bombarded by negative press and all the bad things that happen in life; the natural disasters, the murders, the famines, the political turmoil, just to name a few. But we need to remember that every day, good things are happening all over our world.

Mothers are taking care of their sick children, fathers are working double shifts to support their families, and children are making their parents proud of them. Individual efforts count. Our challenge is to make the world a happier place through our own unselfish efforts, day in and day out.

The past can shape our future, but it cannot be our future. Our individual efforts can make the world a little brighter for ourselves, our families, and our communities. The simple things we do to help others add up over a lifetime. Hopefully, at the end of the game, we have enough points on the board to win the big prize: eternal life.

Rule 4: Your Actions Define You

We have all met people who talk a good game. But when things get tough, they often vacate the field and go home. People will remember us not so much for what we say, but rather for what we do and how we make them feel. I can remember very few words my father spoke to me. But I sure remember what he did for me.

I had a Catholic nun, Sister Mary Joseph, teach me in kindergarten. She wore her black habit, or headdress, every day. We said prayers before school and went to Mass. Blessed Sacrament School was very old. I still remember the dark corridors, the old chalkboards, and the wooden student desks. I really enjoyed kindergarten and Sister Mary Joseph. She made learning fun and never yelled or screamed at anyone. She was very calm and very funny.

My first-grade teacher was Mrs. Yeltsin. She was the worst teacher I ever had in school. She yelled out all her instructions. She was shaped like a pear and had stringy black hair. She reminded me of the Wicked Witch of the East in the Wizard of Oz movie. When the class got a little noisy, Mrs. Yeltsin would take out her ruler and bang it on the chalkboard. She always said, "Stop now, or you'll get a piece of this." That ruler scared me. More than once, she had used it on the backsides of students who misbehaved or did not follow her directions.

One day after lunch, she walked up to my desk and said, "Your work is horrible, Michael." I remember being terrified that she would hit me with that ruler. She did a few days later. I got whacked hard across my fingers for sloppy work.

When I got home that night, Mom knew something was wrong and I finally told Dad what had happened. He said he would take me to school the following morning and talk to the principal. When we arrived at my school the following day, Dad and I went straight to the principal's office. My dad was very quiet and said very little on the walk to the office. Once inside, my dad ruled that principal! I still remember him saying, "Get her in here now." Mrs. Yeltsin came into the office a few minutes later. Dad told her that she would never hit me again with her hand, a ruler, or anything else.

Sometimes the only way out of a situation is to stand up to a bully. Dad stood up to Mrs. Yeltsin in order to protect me and the other kids in her classroom. He was a man of few words; he let his actions speak for him.

Taking action against bullying and standing up for what you believe requires action. Usually, you can't talk a bully down. It was my dad's actions that told me everything I needed to know about his character as a man.

Another person in my childhood who took action to protect me was Justine, our family babysitter. She was an African

American lady who was very friendly and kind. When Mom and Dad went out at night for dinner or to a party, we had Justine come over to watch all of us.

Justine was very protective. She always watched out for us and told us stories about her childhood in Birmingham, Alabama. It was 1961 and back then African Americans had no civil rights. They were separated from whites in housing, restaurants, motels, and in schools. Everywhere you looked there were separate facilities for African Americans. Things started changing in the mid-1960s when Civil Rights laws were passed in our country.

One day, a friend and I found a dead pigeon on the road. My friend wanted to take the pigeon and put it in the mailbox of one of our really mean neighbors. The neighbor was a guy named Mr. Heston. He and his wife were always yelling at the kids for playing in front of their house. The Hestons had no children.

So, my friend put the dead pigeon in the Hestons' mailbox. That night, while Justine was watching us, Mrs. Heston knocked on our front door. Justine answered the bell. Mrs. Heston said, "*What time tomorrow does Michael want to get locked up in Juvenile Hall for the dead pigeon he put in my mailbox? I know he did it with his friend. Someone saw them do it. He is going to pay for this and get some jail time.*" What? Was I really going to jail? I know I did something wrong, but going to jail scared me.

Justine saved me from Mrs. Heston. She told Mrs. Heston, "*Michael was wrong and he will apologize, but he is not going to jail. Now, get out of here.*" It took great courage for an African

American lady to stand up to a white lady in 1961. It was Justine's "Rosa Parks" moment. I did apologize to the Hestons and cleaned their mailbox up. Dad was really upset. I was punished and could not play with my friends for two weeks.

I went into the Marine Corps in 1972 and attended a school called "The Basic School." On the first day of class, all the lieutenants had to pick a roommate. We had one African American officer, Lieutenant Freddy Smith, in our class. After a few minutes everyone, except Freddy, was paired up with a roommate. I picked Freddy to be my roommate and we lived together for a year.

Freddy became a very good friend. He got out of the Marine Corps and went into business. I think I picked Freddy because of what Justine did for me that day back in 1961. I've learned not to judge people by their skin color, or their religion, or anything else that makes them different. Everyone is the same inside. Try to judge each person by their character. Surround yourself with people of good character and you will become a better person. Be a person of action and stand up for what you believe.

In high school, my daughter, Kerrie, played all positions on her travel baseball team and developed into a pretty good pitcher. Just like parents can be brutal to the kids on the field with their comments, coaches can also be vindictive and petty. There are many bullies in life. One game stands out to me.

Kerrie had started the game and by the 4th inning, it was clear to everyone in the bleachers that she had lost her pitching control. She was pitching in the dirt about two feet from the plate. The coach kept her in the game. "Come on, Kerrie, get with the program," he kept saying to her over and over again. Kerrie started crying. "That's not going to work. You have to get yourself out of the jam you put yourself in." I could not believe what I was hearing. Dana had to hold me back from charging into the dugout. I kept thinking about the way Dad had rescued me from Mrs. Yeltsin back in first grade.

Kerrie struck out another batter and came into the dugout completely broken. The moment the game ended, I charged onto the field. I got in this coward's face and said, *"If you ever make my little girl cry again, I will make you cry."* He backed down and apologized.

To this day, Kerrie reminds me about the time I faced off with her coach. I protected her then, and I will always protect her. She will always be my baby girl. Kerrie will remember what I did for her, not what I said.

My point is very simple; don't talk about what you would do, just do it. Be a person of action. If you do not take the wheel and drive your own life, someone else will. A lot of people sat on the sidelines during the 1930s in Nazi Germany. Still more people sat it out in the 1960s when racial segregation was tearing our country apart. Today, the country is divided more than at any time in my lifetime. We need to continually pray for God's help to keep us on the path that leads to light, not darkness.

Strive to be part of the solution, not part of the problem. Get involved and take on the bullies in the world. You will feel better knowing you did the right thing by not looking the other way. Take action and stand up for yourself and your beliefs.

Rule 5: Shape Your Own Character

Faith, morality, and character form the bedrock of our lives. Each element impacts our behavior. If we have a set of standards, we have a roadmap to live our lives. If we have no moral compass and have not been taught right from wrong, we can easily run off the road and crash.

Before Dad died he said a few things to me. I don't remember his exact words, but as best as I can recall, the conversation was as follows:

"Mike, remember the harder you work, the luckier you will get. Don't look back, look forward. Avoid falling into the "everybody else is doing it" trap. You become a liability to your team when you sit on the fence and do nothing."

The terms "honorable" and "righteous" are words seldom heard in our everyday conversations. The Founding Fathers talked about pledging their "sacred honor" when they signed the Declaration of Independence. The Old and New Testaments both talk about the qualities of "righteous" people. Honorable people keep their word, reach out to help others in times of need, and treat people fairly. They exhibit integrity in all their undertakings.

In today's world, you do not hear the word "character" used too often. In fact, most people exhibit good character even though they cannot really describe it in words. The words are: honest, respectful, responsible, caring, and fair. If our parents instill these traits in us early in life through their example, we will have positive modeling to help keep the wheel straight when we hit the potholes in life.

One day when I was six, we went into a bookstore and I saw a book on Medieval Knights. It was full of really cool pictures of knights fighting with swords, jousting on horses, medieval castles, and some really cool stuff. I loved it and asked Mom if I could have it. She said it was too expensive. I could not get the book out of my mind. I just had to have it.

The next Sunday after church, I saw an old lady with a cane on the other side of the street. She was not sure when she could cross the street and she seemed very confused. I thought it might be a good idea to help her cross the street. I remember thinking, If I do a good deed, maybe Mom and Dad will get me that book. So, I bolted across the street and grabbed her gently by the arm. I escorted her across the street and got her safely to the other side. What a good deed, I thought to myself. The old lady thanked me and then she went into our church.

On the way home, I asked my mom about the book. I figured in my six-year-old head that my good deed should be rewarded. I deserved that book on Medieval Knights. Wrong! Mom looked back at me and said, *"Michael, just because you do something good does not mean you get something good in return. You do good things to help other people. Don't expect to get any rewards just because you do the right things in life."* Mom's words made little sense to me at the time. As I got older, I realized why she said that. Don't expect any rewards in life. Do things that help other people because it is the right thing to do. Your reward is feeling better about yourself.

There are a lot of good deeds in life that go unnoticed. Don't expect a pat on the back every time you do something good. My mom's way of saying it was, *"Do good and good things will come back your way."*

In the Marine Corps, they teach young Marines the Leadership Traits and Principles. The traits include: decisiveness, tact, judgment, initiative, loyalty, and integrity. It is drilled into your head (brain-housing group as we Marines say) by your Drill Instructors. The most important leadership trait is integrity; the trait of being honest with yourself and others. The worst thing you can be accused of as a leader is to have committed an integrity violation, meaning you lied or did something dishonest. It is a big thing in the Marine Corps to be accused of an integrity violation. Entire careers can be destroyed on a single event if you violate the sacred trust your leaders place in you.

Your character will not be measured by how well you stay on top, but rather how you bounce off the bottom in life. True character is measured in times of crisis. It is easy to talk about how you would handle a certain situation in a classroom setting. But when you are in the cockpit and actually flying the mission, things look different.

In leading men and women, your character is evaluated every day. Do you throw others under the bus if things go wrong? Do you avoid making decisions and always have an excuse for not getting something done? Do you fail to give an accurate picture of the facts? Do you tell half-truths? Worst of all, are you a "Do as I say, not as I do" type? Just knowing you gave your best should be your reward. Our former president Ronald Reagan put it this way, *"There is no limit to what a person can accomplish in this life, as long as they don't mind who gets the credit."*

The personal rewards that have mattered the most to me in life have been people-focused. I will never forget bumping into Tommy Stroman. He was in my first platoon back in 1973. Tommy was from the South, a high school drop-out, and a problem drinker. He went UA (unauthorized absence) a lot and had numerous conduct violations. He was always on restriction and being fined for his misconduct violations.

Tommy was quiet and always seemed nervous. I finally got through to him and talked him into taking reading courses. He learned to read. He also turned himself in and got help with his alcohol-related issues. Tommy got back on track and made Corporal before he left the platoon. He realized his character flaws, asked for help, and changed the trajectory of his life.

In 1989, I ran into Tommy in the parking lot of a grocery store in northern Virginia. We were up in Burke for one of Matt's soccer games. I was walking out of a food store and heard the words, "Lieutenant Sullivan." The person approaching me looked vaguely familiar. As he got closer, I recognized Tommy Stroman. He was married, had three kids, and was the assistant manager of the grocery store. He told Dana what a positive influence the second platoon Marines and I had on his life. At that moment, I realized how lucky I was to have crossed paths in life with this man of character.

The truth is, whatever doesn't kill you makes you stronger. If you accept failure as a learning opportunity and always do your best, your character will shine through. If you try to do the honest and honorable thing in times of crisis, your behavior will set the standard for others to emulate. You only get to live your life once. Set your expectations bar high for yourself and others. Strive to be a person of integrity and upright character.

Rule 6: Define Your Own Success

Success is a journey, not a destination. If you stop learning and developing your character, you might as well get off the road of life. Once you achieve a goal, you need to recalibrate your life and move on to the next challenge. Your self-satisfaction will come from constantly seeking new opportunities and never letting fear dictate your forward movement.

Fear is a real problem with moving forward in your life. Anxiety and fear of failure can cripple all your efforts to move forward. Anxiety, coupled with uncertainty, can lead to total chaos. There are volumes written on how to overcome your anxiety; there is no one-size-fits-all solution.

Achieving excellence comes when you stare down your fears. Sometimes you need to just "take off." Surfing is a good example. You have all the essential elements: physical challenge, Mother Nature, and unpredictability. How you work with these elements determines your success or failure. Take off too early on a wave and you wipe out and go over the falls. If you hesitate on taking off and back away, you can also get hurt. But if you are confident and just take off and go, nine times out of ten you will make the wave and be successful.

The path to success in life is difficult at times, but worth it when you feel that sense of accomplishment. My brother, Jim, is a martial arts expert who often tells me that he does not want an easy life. He wants a life where his inner strength gets him through the tough times. Never fear failure—it is part of life. Fear not having the courage to get back up when you are knocked down.

Too many people today are crowd followers. They define themselves by how many Facebook friends they have. They are glued to the Internet. Whatever news they read becomes their reality. Critical thinking is some abstract concept. Oftentimes, they have no sense of direction because they have never been taught goal setting.

Our secular society has actually hampered individual growth development. We have become a "nation of sheep," following whoever has the best public relations blitz. We have become so politically correct in our thinking; we are afraid to take a stand on many critical issues. God has become a meaningless concept to many. We try to please "all the people all the time," which Phineas Barnum, the founder of Barnum and Bailey Circus, said was an impossibility.

Don't be defined by others. No matter what you do in life, if it is honest work, it is dignified. If you buy into what others say about you, you will dig a big hole filled with your own self-doubt. If you stand up for what you believe, you will win your self-respect. Your self-respect is essential to your success. Know your weaknesses and seek self-improvement. Accept your faults and embrace change. If you are moving in a positive direction, success will come. And, success breeds more success. The harder you try, the luckier you will be.

Measuring your success will evolve and change over the course of your life. When I was playing baseball, I defined success as going two for three at bat. In school, it was grades and doing my best. As a father, it was raising my children and giving them direction and guidance. In the Marines, it was accomplishing the mission. Today, at seventy-one, I see my success as being the best father, husband, and grandfather I can be.

Everyone is afraid of something. Conquering your fears is essential to your own personal growth and success. I'm reminded of the following childhood story:

Just before starting kindergarten, I got real scared of going to school. Something about going to school scared me. We had a school bus stop around the corner to our house. On the first day of school, Mom walked me to the bus stop, and then she left. I did not want to go to school, so I hid behind some bushes just as the bus arrived. After the bus left, I walked back home. I rang the doorbell and told my mom, "I missed the bus." We only had one car, so she could not take me to school.

The next day, I did the same thing. Mom was mad and called the school to complain about the bus driver leaving me behind. The next day, a neighbor came by and told my mom that I was hiding behind the bushes just before the bus arrived and that the bus driver never saw me. My mom did not get mad. She put her arms around me and told me she would help me get on the bus the next day. And she did.

We walked to the bus stop together the next morning. She told me how scared she was every time my dad flew his jet. Mom said it was ok to be afraid of things in life. She also convinced me how much fun I would have in my new school. I believed her and I got on that bus that day and every day for the rest of my life.

It is better to fail than never to have tried to make something of yourself. As Teddy Roosevelt often said, and I paraphrase, "It is not the critic who counts, the one who points out where the doer of deeds could have done better. The credit belongs to the man who is actually in the arena, who actually strives to do deeds, who spends himself in a worthy cause and in the end triumphs in achievement."

Sacrificing and giving to others will lead to personal satisfaction and success in life. I have little time for self-absorbed people who only care about their own creature comforts. Success is best measured by what you give others, not what you take from them. Every positive role model in my life has been a giver, not a taker.

Rule 7: Try Not to Get in Over Your Head

We all have limitations in life. William Shakespeare, the famous British playwright, once said, "To thy own self be true." We need to recognize when we need to stop, take a breath, and redirect our lives. There are critical pivot points in life. If you stop and change direction, you recover. If you don't stop, you can crash. I learned about my own physical limitations in the summer of 1966.

Before my senior year of high school, Dad bought me my first surfboard. It was a Gordon and Smith nine-foot longboard. I spent every day at the beach that summer trying to master standing up. I remember my first wave like it was yesterday. I surfed with a buddy, Sam, who had been surfing for a few years. At six foot, four inches tall, he was extremely athletic.

Sam and I were very close during my senior year. I went to three different high schools. I know first-hand what a challenge it is to start a new school. I will always remember Sam's kindness and the way he befriended me. No one wants to be alone without friends to talk to during lunch. Sam and I had lunch every day and he introduced me to a lot of guys who also surfed. I now had an identity on campus.

We surfed every weekend. I made one of the worst decisions of my life in November of 1966. There was a huge swell hitting the beaches in San Diego that year and all my friends, including Sam, wanted to paddle out and get some really big waves. I had only been surfing for about six months, but when you are young and inexperienced, you sometimes make really bad decisions.

When we got to the beach, we were in a deep fog bank. The fog had crept along the entire coastline. I wanted to return home, but my friends convinced me to hang around to see if the fog bank cleared, and it did about fifteen minutes later.

What I saw in the ocean was unbelievable. Huge waves were breaking about five hundred yards off the shoreline. To this day, I can see those huge mountains of water exploding off the shore. Every one of us was afraid of backing down and losing face with the crowd on the beach waiting to see us paddle out. We paddled out and it was a big mistake.

It took Sam and me at least a half-hour to make it to the outside where a handful of surfers were setting up for their waves. I saw the whites of their eyes and could see the concern each of them had for the conditions. Some of these guys were really good, but each one had that "deer in the headlights" look.

The waves were very far apart, about 30 seconds between set waves, and easily twenty feet in height. Once I joined the line-up, I noticed something really big coming at us from the outside. We all started to paddle towards this monster wave before it broke on us. I made it over the first wave in the set and looked behind me to see surfboards flinging high in the sky. Guys were bailing their boards and diving as deep as they could into the water. None of the boards had leashes in the 1960s and if you lost your board, you made the swim.

The second wave in the set was in sight. I scrambled, using all my paddling strength to make it over the top. I made it over only to see another monster starting to break right in front of me. It was useless. I had to ditch my board and dive deep.

I was too scared to even think about my circumstances. When I surfaced, I didn't see any of my friends. It was every man for himself at this point. To make things worse, I also noticed that the fog bank was returning. A half-mile offshore in huge surf in a fog bank with no board to float me. Scary!

I was fighting through my fear by focusing on just one thing: seeing my mom and dad again. I prayed. The swim to shore took over forty-five minutes. I calmed myself using a breaststroke and taking long, deep breaths. "A man has to know his limitations," as John Wayne, the famous cowboy actor, would say. It wasn't my time. I am still here. But I don't go out in big surf anymore.

We all get scared in life. Sometimes, it is justified, like when someone is shooting at you. Other times, we need to just calm down and think things through. In the Marine Corps, we called it "presence of mind." Presence of mind is acting in the presence of an unexpected emergency. When we are confronted by a situation and let fear take over, we seldom accomplish anything positive. We don't move forward. We get stuck.

Everyone gets in over their head in life. We face physical, mental, and spiritual challenges that can overwhelm us and consume all our energy. This is when we need to slow down, take deep breaths, and just swim to shore. The waves are big and they're all around us. We may even be in a fog bank. If we stay focused, we can make it to shore.

If things get really bad, we need to ask for help. Sometimes, we get so confused we can't even identify the cause of our fear. In and out of uniform, I have seen people who try to "suck it up" and remain strong. Sometimes it works. More often than not, these people finally break. Ask for help!

Reaching out to your higher power works one hundred percent of the time. Our timeline may not be in sync with God's, but there is a plan to guide us through the darkness. Be patient and let God drive once in a while. What have you got to lose?

Rule 8: Have Some Humility

There is nothing worse than a person who always has all the answers and never makes a mistake. Growing up, we called the kids who always wanted the pats on the back, "Glory Hounds."

Usually these kids were the loudest on the team and always wanted the ball. They were the first to take credit for the win, or blame someone else for the loss. Obnoxious is an understatement in describing their behavior. Guess what, more often than not, they grew up to be obnoxious, self-centered adults. I worked for a few of these people in and out of uniform.

At the opposite end of the spectrum, you will find the quiet, unsung heroes. These kids let their efforts on the field speak to their abilities. They were the first to own up to their mistakes, and never had a problem admitting it was their fault if they struck out. These kids were humble; they possessed the quality of humility. They were patient, non-pretentious, and not self-seeking.

I always looked for humility in the people who worked for me and their ability to say, "I'm sorry, that was my fault." Anyone you know who cannot say these words most likely lacks humility. If you lack humility, you will probably not make it in the military or in the business world. Both are team sports and egotistical, self-centered people just slow the team down.

A humble person is patient and does not get frustrated with the imperfections they see in others. They seldom criticize. Humble people don't have all the answers and go out of their way to seek the truth. A humble person recognizes their own limitations and readily assists others on and off the field. Most importantly, humble people see the beauty in life and take nothing for granted.

My deceased son, John, possessed a high degree of humility. Like my dad, John was quiet and unassuming. Even as a child, he went out of his way to be kind and to help out his friends. When John was your friend, you had a friend for life.

John was proud of his accomplishments, but he never bragged. Like my father, he was more interested in what was going on in your life. He was a good listener and when he gave advice it was solid. John graduated meritoriously from Marine boot camp and received the Navy Achievement Medal while on active duty. We found out about both accomplishments after the fact. Throughout his life, like his brother and sister, he was a giver. He never took himself that seriously and was always there to lend a hand when others needed help. He was a good man.

Pride, the opposite of humility, is a two-edged sword. Taking pride in your achievements and developing self-confidence is a good trait. But too much pride can lead to social friction, an egotistical demeanor, and you becoming a victim of your own bloated self-image. You get full of yourself. You are always right. It is always somebody else who is to blame. I am sure you get the picture; not a good way to win the hearts and minds of others.

Perhaps the humblest man I ever met was Charles Westgate. In my senior year of high school, I got my first job delivering hot chicken dinners in a styrofoam box on the back of my Honda 50 motorcycle. Dad bought me the Honda with the three hundred dollars that he had received from his father's life insurance policy.

Charles Westgate always wanted to be called "Wes." Wes was a sheet metal worker at a local aircraft plant. He had a wife and three kids, all under ten. He was barely thirty and was losing his hair. Wes worked forty hours a week at the plant and another forty at the chicken take out store he managed. He worked seven days a week and had little time for his family. His wife worked in the restaurant and she often brought the kids with her to work. It was chaotic, with all the kids running around the kitchen, drivers picking up orders, and customers yelling out menu items. Wes never broke a sweat. He just handled things in a cool, calm, collected fashion.

Wes always looked tired, but he presented an immaculate personal appearance and was always friendly. I never heard him complain, not once. He took good care of me and the other workers and always paid us on time. He seldom talked about himself, but he did let us know he was a Marine in the

1950s. He was very proud of his service and would tell us stories about his boot camp experiences at Paris Island. Wes was an honorable man.

Mr. Westgate always said, *"Complaining gets you nowhere in life; just handle it."* He also said, *"Don't be like me. Work smart, not hard, and get an education. Don't drop out like I did."*

Having Wes say this to me reinforced what my dad had been saying for years about the importance of a college education. I decided to get a college degree.

Rule 9: Keep your Headspace in Balance

The spiritual, mental, and physical components of our lives need to be in sync. Stress comes about when we are out of balance. Each day, I try to say a prayer, read something to improve my mental awareness, and conduct some type of physical exercise. Many studies have highlighted the correlation between physical exercise and emotional well-being. I know first-hand that physical fitness can lift you up from the depths of depression.

When I came back from my Lebanon tour in the mid-1980s, I suffered from periods of deep depression. Despite my success as a Marine officer and having a beautiful family, I was not a happy camper. My stress level was in overload.

My mind got stuck on thinking about my past failures, and I got to the point I really hated my job and going to work. It seemed that every day, something else was going wrong in my life. I quit physical exercise because I was always too busy with my job. I got to the point where my negativity began to take over my being. Drinking became a problem. I tried to self-medicate myself out of depression.

When you are depressed, your headspace gets in a "do-loop." No matter how hard you try, you go negative and you go negative often. The self-talk you experience is like a revolving door. You keep going in circles, "worst casing" every aspect of your life. The gloom and doom thoughts you experience put you in a frozen mental state where you cannot accomplish even basic tasks. You wonder if others can see your distress and the negative thoughts are going through your mind. You pretend everything is fine and it becomes a nightmare. You have to dig yourself out of this hole, but you do not know how to break the chains of depression.

I finally surrendered and went to see a psychologist on base. I was brought up to be a self-reliant person and going to a shrink to ask for help was really hard for me. After several sessions, the doc convinced me to go back to a vigorous exercise program. I remember him telling me how important it was to experience the endorphins that come from strenuous physical activity. More importantly, he explained to me how critical it was that I complete a daily task from start to finish. I quit drinking and began to say my prayers more often.

The most important thing he said to me was, "*Inch by inch life is a cinch, yard by yard life is hard. Start doing little things right and everything else will fall into place.*" My disorganized life came into focus. I was trying to get everything done and nothing was getting done. I began the simple process of each night visualizing the next day's tasks. I prioritized the tasks, making sure I carved out time for physical training. I got myself into a success cycle and I quit saying, "I can't."

My balance wheel eventually got recalibrated. It took months, but the result was a happier, more productive Mike Sullivan. Having experienced my own depression and alcohol addiction, it became easier for me to recognize these conditions when they affected my Marines. I became a more understanding leader. I became a lot humbler.

When the stresses of life come, you are more often than not ill-prepared. It is like sailing on a still ocean and suddenly a rogue wave capsizes your boat. Reactions to stress can take many forms, including anger and denial. If you let stress take over your life, it will. Prayer is essential, but taking action is also critical to recovery. Taking action includes identifying the cause of your stress and getting the facts. If you have the facts, you can reduce uncertainty, which in turn reduces your stress.

At the end of the day, most of the stress we experience in life is self-inflicted. We let our perceptions, not facts, take over our thinking. Social media is a case in point. If we let Facebook become our reality, we are setting ourselves up for that crash. If the perpetually happy pictures we post begin to represent our reality, we wash away our real challenges in life. Life is not meant to be a series of iPhone shots. These project an impression, not the reality of our lives.

Today, someone criticizes us on Facebook and *bam* we take it personally and often overblow their comments. We struggle with getting even, setting the record straight, and letting our other social media friends know that we are right. In short, we get addicted to a world that may have an adverse impact on our own self-image. Reality gets bent.

You are what you put between your ears. You cannot control other people, places, or things. But you can control what you watch on the Internet, read, and listen to. You can control who you choose to be your friends and colleagues. Seek the truth by critically thinking your way through the issue. With truth, you will be able to reduce your life-stressors to bite-size challenges that you can more easily handle.

My last point, "You have to learn to juggle cotton balls in a windstorm." You will always have multiple priorities, deadlines, relationship issues, and setbacks to deal with each and every day. The world is filled with imperfections; it was designed that way. Keep focused on what is really important: your family and your faith.

Grandpa John, Joan and I 1959

Grandpa Stiles, War Hero 1917

Mom and Dad 1972

Jim, Matt, Dad, John and me in 1982

Marine Corps Ball 1994

Private First Class John Sullivan and me 1994

Dana's Mom and Dad, Bill and June Rudershausen 2003

Matt surfing big wave in Mexico

Grandpa Bill and Ayden

John and Jen with Ayden and Ava hiking 2013

Sullivan Walk in honor of Grandpa John 2010

2012 Disneyland trip with Ava and Ayden

2012 family picture in Kauai

The family with Matt and Katy's first son,
Michael Matthew, 2013

John and his kids Ava and Ayden 2014

Ayden and Ava with Nana and Papa on two vacations;
Alaska and New York City

New York

Matt had this brick placed near the Oceanside pier to honor his brother

Kerrie and Bryan with their children:
Emma Grace and Hunter William

Matt and Katy with their children: Michael Matthew, Katherin Quinn, Sarah Jacqueline, and Ryan William

All the grandkids reunited in 2020 at Mission Bay

Rule 10: Family Tragedies are a Part of Life

When I was in fifth grade, I saw a really bad helicopter crash. I was riding my bike with my friend Jimmy on a Saturday morning when we saw black smoke rising from a grass field near our house. We peddled over to the field and saw several ambulances and fire trucks already at the scene. There was no sign that any of the men inside the helo had survived. Later in the day, my dad told me that the pilot and copilot had died in the crash. My dad seemed really upset.

That night we found out that the pilot, Lieutenant Appleton, died in the crash. He and his wife and their four children lived around the corner from our house.

The next day, I saw a lot of cars parked at the Appletons' house. One car was a black sedan with an official Navy logo painted on the side. The Appleton kids stayed inside their house for about a week. Everyone, including my mom, brought food over for them to eat.

When the Appleton kids went back to school, everyone felt really sorry for them. Jimmy Appleton was in fifth grade too, but not in my class. No one knew what to say to any of the Appletons. I could not imagine what it would be like to lose my dad. A year later, the family moved back to Tennessee where Mrs. Appleton's mom and dad lived.

I learned in fifth grade that life can be short. My dad tried to explain it to me in a few words, "Bad things happen to good people. Life is not fair, Michael. Tragedy occurs every day."

In 1991, I was assigned as the senior Marine for a reserve unit in Tampa, Florida. Our unit was deployed to Saudi Arabia in preparation for Operation Desert Storm. On December 5th I received word from my headquarters to make a condolence call on a young widow who was living in Fort Myers, Florida. Her husband was a Marine serving in the Persian Gulf. He was killed in a tragic accidental shooting involving another Marine.

A condolence call is a sacred duty for a Marine officer. Condolence calls are made in person and always by an officer. There is nothing more difficult than telling the next of kin that their son or daughter is not coming home. There are guidelines for the call, but no script. You take a navy chaplain and a navy corpsman along with you when you conduct the condolence call.

It was a three-hour drive from Tampa to Fort Myers. I had the accident report and a few details about the incident. I knew that the family would have many questions. I also knew that I would not have all the answers. On the way down, I thought about my dad and the condolence calls he made when other pilots were killed in aircraft training accidents. Dad always said that it was the hardest thing he ever did.

When we arrived at the address, it was six o'clock in the morning. Regulations state that you make the call at the earliest available time. We were in a black sedan with a Navy official seal on the passenger's door. It reminded me of the sedan that pulled up to the Appleton's house so long ago. Another officer had to tell Mrs. Appleton that her husband would not be coming home that day.

I thought I saw someone open the front curtains in the house. I knew someone was up, so I made the decision to knock on the front door. My mind was racing, but I knew I would find the right words when the time came. I was not prepared for what I saw when the front door opened. The young wife was in a bathrobe and obviously in the late stages of pregnancy. She looked at me in my Dress Blues and then she saw the chaplain. She knew. Just then the Marine's parents came into the living room. The wife had been staying with them, since she was due to have her baby in the next few days.

I remember having everyone sit down on the couch and I began telling them what happened. Somehow the words came to me. It was one of the saddest moments of my life. I explained how and when her husband's body would return, as well as the military burial ceremony. The deceased's father had served in the military. He was strong, but I could see how broken he was. I tried the best I could to comfort the family. I remember thinking how horrible it would be to lose a son or a daughter. Parents are not supposed to bury their children. Today, I know first-hand the pain of losing a child.

I coordinated the support for the funeral service. Hundreds of people showed up to pay their respects for our Marine and his family. The military ceremony ended with the playing of taps and a rifle salute. I presented the flag to the young wife with the words, "On behalf of a grateful nation, I present this flag to you in remembrance of your husband's devoted service." Bad things happen to good people in this life. I knew it then, and I know it now.

I lost my mom from a stroke in 2002. Prior to her death, she was hospitalized for a few days in a comatose state. On the afternoon of May 22nd my dad called me and told me to get to the hospital as soon as possible. I arrived at the hospital with Dana around 2 pm. All the immediate family was gathered in the hospital room. Mom looked fragile, but very calm. Her hand was at her side slightly overhanging the side of her bed. I held her hand for a few minutes. I felt her gently squeeze my hand and then she died. I believe in divine intervention and that life is a series of miracles. God let me feel my mother's love one last time before she entered heaven. My dad wept and cried out to all of us, "We have lost her." My father's words struck me deeply.

My dad died in 2007. He died on March 17th, Saint Patrick's Day. A week before he died, the family gathered in his home to say good-bye. He was days from death. My last words to my father were, "Dad, I love you."

As I looked at John Sullivan for the last time, I remembered the words in a letter from his friend sent to him shortly after Mom died. *"I know this has not been an easy time for you,*

Sully. Sometimes it seems God puts the burden on those most able to handle it. That you have always done, Sully. I know of no one that I respect and care about more. Thinking back over fifty years, I remember our tour on the Bon Homme Richard carrier. You and your maintenance crew were always there most of the night keeping those birds flying—then flying yourself the next day. Thank you for letting us know of Mary's passing."

Like a true fighter pilot, Dad faced his death with great courage. He never took the morphine for the pain during his last days. He faced death with great dignity and "took the pain." In many respects, it was Dad's defining moment; his last "qual" day. I miss his words of encouragement, his wise counsel, and his love.

On the evening of January 10th 2017, Dana and I were pulling into our garage following a ten-day vacation to Saint John's Island in the Caribbean. As we rounded the corner to our house, we saw a lot of cars parked at Kerrie's house. She lives right around the corner from us. As we unpacked our bags in the garage at about 11 pm, my son Matt walked up our driveway and hugged me. Kerrie grabbed Dana and then the words came out of Matt; "We have lost him."

We both asked, "How?" How did we lose John, what do you mean we lost John? Was it an accident? Then my son Matt uttered the words that no parent should ever hear; "John hung himself." At that moment in time, I knew that our lives would never be the same. I can still see my wife on the floor, sitting helplessly with our daughter trying to console her. I got down on one knee and repeatedly made the sign of the cross. No one could have comforted Dana or me at that moment.

There are no words to describe losing a child so suddenly and so senselessly. It was like a gut punch, an emotional nuclear blast. I was mad as hell. How could John do this to his family? I did not know the circumstances surrounding John's death; we were all blindsided. No one saw it coming. None of us suspected that John was in so much pain that he would end his life.

The Sullivans had never suffered a loss like this. My life has had its ups and downs, but we always weathered the storm as a family. Taking one's life is something that not only causes pain and grief, but it also has the potential to tear the family apart. None of us are ever prepared for this type of tragedy.

I knew instinctively that this was the pivotal moment of my life and that all of our lives would be changed forever. I also knew that everything I had ever learned about love, faith, forgiveness, and compassion would lead us from this darkness back to the light. I knew that blame would destroy our family, and I knew deep down that only John could have prevented this tragedy. Many people reached out to help. None of us lacked for food the week following John's death. Neighbors prepared meals and the family gathered daily to share their grief. Everyone was dealing with the loss differently. We were all in some state of shock.

Jim, my brother, and I spent hours trying to figure out what happened. Bryan, who had seen John almost daily for the two weeks prior to his death, was looking for signs or clues that John was depressed. Matt was heartbroken and tried to console Dana as best he could. Kerrie opened up her house to everyone and tried to stay busy with her own son, Hunter. We all talked endlessly about the circumstances, trying to find answers that never came. We all realized that, for whatever reason, John had taken his life and left behind a widow and two beautiful children. The reality set in for all of us.

I remember reaching out to Matt Giacolone, Katy's dad, one night shortly after John's death. Matt is a wonderful, caring, and thoughtful man. I value his opinion on many things and he is truly a man of character. Matt listened and I tried to reason out why John had taken his life. I remember Matt's words; "John had a blind spot. The right combination of things were happening in his life that made him do what he did. We all have blind spots and no one could have seen this coming. No one could have done anything differently. We will never know the truth about his blind spot."

When I told my brother Jim that John had taken his life on the morning of January 11th, he wailed. He and John were very close. He reached out to me that day, as he continues to do every day. We can talk about things at a very deep emotional level. He is my best friend and his sage advice has always helped me get through tough times. Jim, like Matt Giacolone, believed that John was not in his normal state of mind when he took his life. Jim called it the "Perfect Storm." Jim said, "It was not just one thing, but probably a combination of factors that caused him to act the way he did."

Before we had John's Celebration of Life, we all gathered at Matt and Katy's house in San Diego. The girls went through hundreds of family pictures, which we placed on huge poster boards. We also took John's old Stewart surfboard and had a picture of him laminated onto it. This was the board you see him riding in all the Mexico trips. God, what a blessing those trips were to Jim, John, Matt, and I. The pictures of all of us riding perfect waves were captured in many photos and will stay in our memories forever.

John's Celebration of Life occurred at 1200 on Monday the 23rd of January. We gathered at our house at about 10:30 am. The wind was howling and about halfway to the church, it hailed ice. It was the worst hail storm any of us had ever experienced. It was as if the heavens were crying for all of us. We expected about a hundred and fifty people to attend the celebration; double that number showed up to honor our son.

The Sullivans, Nours, and Giacolones all attended, as well as neighbors, friends, and many of John's co-workers. Some of John's high school surf buddies also showed up to pay their respects. It was truly amazing to see all the people in that church, so many people who respected my son for his character and friendship.

Our Celebration was conducted by a young pastor who did a magnificent job with the eulogy. Several family members spoke about John's life and his impact on others including Fred Nour, Uncle Jim, Uncle Bill, Matt, Bryan, Don Burns, and myself.

My remarks were as follows:

"Thank you all for being here today.

Families come together in times of crisis and tragedy. I want all of you to know that the Sullivans will make it through this challenge. All of us still see the light and the good that was in my son. We all know that love, understanding, and above all faith will pull us through this tragedy.

We know that John is now in the hands of the Lord and that he will continue to touch us all in the quiet moments of our life.

We measure life not in minutes or hours, but rather in the totality of the years we spend on this earth. We are all grateful to have had John with us for over forty years.

We are grateful to be able to remember how he loved the water and the surf. From playing on the beaches of Waikiki as a baby, to surfing waves with his brother Matt, Uncle Jim, and Trey McGriff in Mexico. John was most at peace in the water.

During his lifetime, we saw how he loved his brother. Matt always had a great friend and protector with John. They roamed dinosaur canyon at Camp Pendleton as youngsters and lived together at the beach before they married. Both my boys married the loves of their lives and raised beautiful children. Jennie and Katy have brought great joy to our lives; Dana and I love both women as we do our own daughter, Kerrie.

From the minute Kerrie was born, John had a little sister to watch over. When I was deployed, John was the man of the house. He loved Kerrie and shared in her great joy when she met Bryan. Bryan was John's best friend. Bryan is our third Sullivan son and a pillar of strength for our entire family.

Kerrie and Bryan have Hunter now. The 'Little Hunter' we all call him. I can still see John calming the little man down and holding him as he would his own children.

We were able to see John's soccer games, his high school graduation, his Marine Corps boot camp graduation, and his marriage to Jennie. We saw his great joy in his eyes when Ayden was born and the way he cuddled Ava when she came into this world.

Dana and I were able to see John almost daily over the past fifteen years. John, Jennie, and the kids lived a few blocks away. We have had too many to count family gatherings.

Dana and John carpooled together and spent countless hours discussing how they could help veterans. Like Forrest Gump would say, "Dana and John went together like peas and carrots." My wife and John both dedicated their lives to helping vets and their families.

Those of us who knew John know how profoundly he loved others. He reached out to those in trouble and willingly did whatever he could to make the lives of those around him easier. He was always there for his family. John did what sons and daughters should all strive to do, he made his parents proud.

His quiet and thoughtful demeanor was evident in all that he did. I remember one incident when he was in the Marine Corps. He received a Navy Achievement Medal as a corporal.

He did not tell me about the award, but I found out about it and stood in the back of the formation to hear the words read on his citation. I was as proud of my son then as I am now. He was a man of great character.

We all need something to believe in when we fall into despair. We all need faith. We all need to understand what happened to my son and learn from this tragedy. Most of all, we all need to remember my son as the devoted husband and father that he was for over forty years. He will be missed by all of us.

When I am alone, I can still see the baby Dana gave me to hold for the first time at the Norton Air Force Base terminal in 1976. I can see him in my backpack as we walked along the beach in Waikiki. I see him and Matt exploring Dinosaur Canyon at Camp Pendleton. I see him as a young Marine. I remember the look on his face when he exchanged vows with Jennie at the Ranch House Chapel; he was radiant with joy and love. Most importantly, I can still see him with his children. He loved Ayden and Ava with his whole being. He was a good man.

When I die and cross over to the other side, both John Sullivans will be there to meet me. Of this, I am certain."

Rule 11: Be Responsible

I developed a deep sense of responsibility from watching my father. My earliest recollection of him was shaving. I was maybe three when I first marveled at the way he effortlessly moved the razor across his face. It was a single blade and very sharp. He never cut himself. He took his time and made sure every whisker was erased from his face. I remember him saying later in life, *"You have to be able to look into the mirror and be happy with what you see."* That was Dad's way of saying, be comfortable in your own skin.

Each year, we got the opportunity to attend his squadron's family events in an old aircraft hangar. My sister and I could climb on all the jets and eat vanilla ice cream. I remember the enlisted sailors always coming over to tell us that Dad was one of the "good officers." At the time, I did not appreciate how great a compliment this was to my dad's leadership abilities.

I was in eighth grade and Dad was stationed at Naval Air Station, Miramar. His plane un-expectantly went into an uncontrolled spin and he bailed out at 10,000 feet. He landed near the Saltan Sea. His legs were both badly crushed when both got lodged between two boulders. My mom and I heard the news on the radio that, "Commander John Sullivan has been involved in a fatal crash near the Saltan Sea." Back in those days, nobody notified the next of kin before reporting accidents and deaths in the news. Until Dad's squadron commander called an hour later, my mom and I thought Dad was dead.

Dad came home with a cast on each leg. He could not breathe that night and was rushed to Balboa Naval Hospital. He had developed blood clots in his lungs and was in serious condition for the next week or so. The hospital was located near Balboa Stadium where the Chargers played before Qualcomm Stadium was built. We played a Pop Warner championship game on a Saturday, which we lost. After the game, I walked to the gate of the hospital, showed my dependents ID card, and found Dad's room in building 26. As I walked in, I was shocked. Dad had lost a lot of weight and looked almost gray in color. He smiled and we talked for a little while. I remember what he said to me that day, "Mike, you have to learn to hit the curveballs in life." I am sure Dad had heard those same words from his own father.

Years later, Dad told me the entire story of his accident. They did a formal accident investigation to uncover the cause. The first draft of the accident report came out identifying two causes for the near-fatal mishap: faulty maintenance and pilot error. The blame was being thrown at the young enlisted men who serviced the aircraft, as well as Dad's inability to control the aircraft when it went into a spin and out of control. Back in those days, the aviation community was really tight, especially amongst fighter pilots. My dad managed to have the report changed before it was published. The final report cited "pilot error" as the sole cause of the crash. No mention was made of the maintenance men who had worked on the aircraft before it took off that day. My dad took full responsibility because he did not want to hurt the careers of the young enlisted Sailors. He took the bullet for his men.

Dad was passed over (not promoted) for captain. The accident hurt his chances of being promoted, even though he was awarded the Bronze Star Medal for his performance during the 1965 Dominican Republic crisis. Dad was never bitter. He retired and did what he always wanted to do. He taught high school business classes for seventeen years. John Sullivan was an honorable man. He did not make captain, but he did attend my promotion ceremony to colonel. I can still see the smile on his face.

Taking responsibility for your own actions seems easy enough. But the world is filled with people who pass the buck. They have a hard time accepting their own failures. It is easier for them to blame some other poor soul for the mistake made. Some people avoid responsibility and they do not want to be in charge. They want to blend in and, as we say in the Marines, "stay off the skyline." As a leader, whether you are a father, mother, teacher, or part of a team, you are responsible for others.

All of us establish our own legacies in life. Many people wander aimlessly, moving from one day to the next. They have an attitude that things will happen and that whatever comes their way they can handle. They relegate their futures to the hand of fate. I would rather take charge of my life, develop a plan, and own it.

We control our own destinies; we should always be ready for that stopwatch to stop ticking. Do you want to be remembered as a kind and generous person, a person of integrity, a loving parent, and an honorable man or woman? Or, as a selfish, uncaring, self-centered individual? Decide early in life what you want your legacy to be and go out and earn it.

Rule 12: Be Grateful

Don't wish for an easy life free from stress. That won't happen. Pray for the strength to endure the hardships that will surely come your way. Don't drown in your own self-pity. The truth is, outside your immediate family and maybe a close friend or two, no one gives a hoot.

I don't like whiners; try not to be one. We are surrounded by people who blame others for their misfortunes. We have too many victims and not enough grateful people in our world. In the Marines, we called these victims "whiners." We can all feel sorry for ourselves; that is easy. But it takes character to get off your pity pot and move forward. Sometimes you have to put things in perspective to appreciate what you have in life. Look around the world; there are lots of broken people who have nothing.

Grateful people are happy people. Period. Ungrateful people consider themselves victims and cannot embrace the joys of life. I count my blessings every day. I am happy. I love seeing my grandchildren play and seeing Dana so happy when she is surrounded by all the kids.

The following stories exemplify, for me, what it means to be grateful.

In second grade, I had a friend named Charlie. He did not have a father and his mother seemed a little weird to me. We played outside a lot. I rarely got invited into Charlie's house. One day, Charlie invited me to dinner.

Charlie lived in an apartment. When I entered through the front door, the first thing I saw was a small kitchen and a lot of dirty dishes piled up around the sink. His mom was sitting in the living room, slumped over in a big gray chair. The living room was really small and very messy.

His mom was watching an old black and white TV and was kind of sleeping. However, her eyes were open. She said, "Why is that boy here?" Charlie told her that he had invited me to dinner. She then said, "We have nothing to eat."

I remember being embarrassed for my friend. He made it seem like it was no big deal, but I know it bothered him. He had eaten at our house on several occasions and my mom was always giving him snacks to eat. I went into his room to play and I immediately noticed how clean his room was. Everything was in its place. We played cars for an hour and then I had to go home. Charlie made sure all the cars were put back in place.

I told my mom about what I had seen in Charlie's house. She told me that some people lived differently than our family did. She also said, "Michael, you are lucky your dad makes enough money to support our family." I was seven years old, but right then I realized that some people were really poor. Charlie's mom did not work and his dad was dead. Charlie did not have all the toys that I had, but he took care of the toys he did have. Despite living in a home that was filthy, he kept his room clean.

Charlie did not have anyone telling him to clean his room or make his bed. He just did these things because he knew that keeping organized was important. Today, I realize that sometimes you have to do things without anyone telling you to do them. Sometimes, you have to set your own example and seek your own path like Charlie did in that messy apartment. Despite Charlie's surrounding chaos, he made his bed every day. He had standards that he lived by and he did what he needed to do to stay organized. Charlie did not have much, but he was grateful.

My second story happened to me in 1976 while serving in Okinawa. I was on a thirteen-month unaccompanied tour. No one was allowed to take their wives or kids overseas in the 1970s. Being away from Dana was tough; I missed her every day. To keep focused, we all worked hard, sometimes seven days a week. Father Joe was our chaplain. Around Christmas time, everyone was getting homesick. A few guys got to take leave, but most of us spent the holidays on the island. One day, Father Joe invited all of us to a Christmas party. He made it seem like it was really going to be a great time. He promised lots of food and drink. Father was no teetotaler, so we suspected lots of beer and whiskey at the event. He did not want any of the officers to drive, so he chartered a bus to take us to this event about ten miles from Camp Schwab.

We traveled to a location about thirty minutes away. When we arrived, we found ourselves in a gated area with several buildings that looked like schoolrooms. We were all a little taken back as the Father told us to get out of the bus and follow him. We all gathered around the bus and awaited his instructions. He told us to wait for the guide who would take us to the party. A few minutes later, we saw a man walking towards us with a cane. As he got closer, I noticed he had rags on his hands and feet. He had no shoes on. The closer he approached, the more I noticed his facial features. He had a stub where his nose should have been. He also had a patch over one eye. This did not feel like a party. Father said, "Yoshoki will show you where the party is, gents."

Once inside one of the buildings, many people came up and greeted us with a polite bow. I saw many rags wrapped around arms, legs, and heads. We were in a leper colony. The leprosy had affected their physical appearance. But, most of these wonderful people greeted us with a smile. Father had planned a party where we were the hosts. There was no alcohol. We handed out baskets of fruit and cookies. We stayed for about an hour. It was really quiet on the bus ride home. We were all still missing home. But Father O'Connor had put things in perspective for all of us. We were grateful.

The last story involves a homeless man I met in 2001. I never knew his last name. "Pinky" ran ten miles a day along the beaches of Oceanside. I ran into him one day after surfing. He was cooling down after a long run. He was shirtless and wearing an old pair of Keds sneakers, not exactly the best running shoes for distance running. I knew he was homeless. He slept under the stairs at Tysons street.

I asked Pinky, "How far do you run?" He did not answer me, but I repeated my question to him. He then said, "Ten miles." I kept seeing him running along the beach each time I surfed. About a month or so later, I ran into him taking a break along the coast highway. I asked him what size shoes he wore. Turns out he was size eight and a half just like me. I reached into my van and asked him if he wanted to try my slightly worn Nike running shoes. He gratefully accepted the shoes.

I saw Pinky running with my old shoes on a few weeks later. I was getting out of the water and he proceeded to tell me how much his running had improved. He thanked me for the shoes.

I never had any long conversations with Pinky. I learned he had a brother living in Oceanside who suffered from Parkinson's disease. He also told me he was forty-four years old. Over the next five years, I kept him supplied with running shoes. He had them all; Nike, Saucony, Brooks, etc. Pinky was always thanking me for the shoes. He always said, "A man needs good support on his feet to go the distance." He was grateful.

I hadn't seen him for a few months and I started asking the locals where Pinky had gone. Some said he moved to Arizona. One day, I learned he had died from a heart attack while running along the beach.

Some people "worst case" their lives. With every little setback, they see gloom and doom. Bad things happen when you become a "professional victim." You stress more and start blaming everything under the sun for your problems. I don't have any problems. Why? A wise friend once told me, "There are no problems in life, Mike, only challenges."

Being grateful for what God has given you in life is important. Grateful people are happy people. I have always tried to inventory what I have in life, not what I lack.

Sometimes we take things for granted. We assume we will be healthy and that we will have what we need in life. We assume our family members will always be there for us. We take for granted our jobs. But, in an instant, you can lose everything. Sometimes we get locked into the future without paying attention to today.

When challenges come your way, look inward to find the answers. Ask others for help. Don't isolate and dig holes; it buys you nothing. Be grateful! Today only comes around once.

Rule 13: Forgive Yourself and Others

To err is human; to forgive is divine. I remember hearing these words at a very young age. I could not comprehend their meaning. What about getting even or an eye for an eye? I heard these phrases as well. This is pretty confusing guidance, no matter what your age.

The worst day of my life was when we heard the news about John on January 10th 2017. For many months, I blamed my son for the horrific pain his actions caused the Sullivan family. How could he be so selfish? What about the kids? How could you do that, John? After all we have done for you? Why couldn't you wait and talk things out with your mom and dad? These questions went through my head twenty-four seven. I dug endless holes for the answers. The answers never came.

What did I not see in John's upbringing? Was I too hard on him? Did I fail to make an emotional connection with him growing up? Was he afraid to come to me? A lot of people in the family let me know what a terrific father I had been. Words like, "You did everything and more for John" were tossed my way.

I also blamed others for John's death. Suffice to say, I was caught up in the blame game for a while. I was trying to be strong for the family, but I fell apart at night in my quiet moments. I focused on the family, just like I did with my Marines.

Through faith, I learned to forgive myself and others. I think I would have drowned in self-pity if I had not changed my focus. I got out of the blame lane and crossed over to the forgiveness lane. It is a daily task to give yourself and others a break. If you don't, you wallow in hate, which will eat you up from the inside out.

Blame and resentment are bedfellows. When you forgive someone, the slate should be wiped clean. You can start over. But oftentimes we harbor resentments when our pride has been hurt. Resentment slowly kills a relationship. On the outside, everything seems normal and back on track, but inside we are simmering with ill will towards the other person. Not good! Resentment is a cancer. If you don't end it, it will spread to others. We start talking to others about how we have been unfairly treated and we spin ourselves up even more. The best advice I ever got on resentment was three words, "Let it go." Pray for forgiveness.

Rule 14: Make Good Decisions

Decision-making and timing go hand in hand. I once worked for a general who waited until the last staff briefing to make his final decision on the plan. He always said, "I need facts, not theories, and hope is not a plan." In making a decision, he wanted to know all the possibilities then decide on the best course of action. He relied on his intuition and experience to decide on the best way forward. He often said, "An eighty percent solution delivered on time is better than a one hundred percent solution delivered after our train leaves the station."

Opportunities are fleeting. In our everyday lives, we have to rely on our intuition and life experiences to make decisions. Failure is the greatest teacher. When we fail, hopefully we learn. Sometimes, we hesitate to make a decision and fail to capture an opportunity. Windows open and windows close. Wisdom comes from making good, as well as bad, decisions. Sometimes, it takes time to determine if a decision is right or wrong.

In 1972, I joined the Marine Corps. The draft was in effect and I received my draft notice in the mail. As a draftee, I would have to spend two years in the army. On the way home from the University of San Diego, Dana suggested looking into officer programs. I was graduating from college in two months. We passed a billboard going down Highway 5 that read, "The Marines are looking for a Few Good Men."

We drove to the San Diego Marine Officer Selection Office. I took a simple test and in two months I was in Quantico, Virginia getting "indoctrinated" by two really mean Drill Instructors. I was on a two-year officer program contract, which was the exact amount of time I would have had to spend in the army as an enlisted draftee. The two-year officer program was deactivated while I was in Officer Candidates School. I was making more money as an officer and, more importantly, I gained great leadership experience working alongside some great leaders. To me, it was great timing.

I also had great timing when I met and later married Dana. I had one date with her when she was in high school. We did not see each other for a year or so. I ran into her at a college bookstore during her freshman year of college and we have been together ever since. A chance meeting that turned into a marriage, three kids, and eight grandchildren. Once again, good timing makes the difference.

A friend of mine once said, "Mike, ninety percent of the things we worry about never happen." I know a lot of people who fall into this category. They try to control every aspect of their lives, and when things do not go their way, they fall apart. In an attempt to control a situation, they often over-think an issue, which makes the situation even worse. Usually, these people fail to get the facts upfront. They react rather than develop a plan to solve the challenge. In the Marine Corps, we refer to this type of leader as a "Ready, shoot, aim" type.

When I think about decision-making, I am reminded of some sage advice given to me by our instructor, Colonel Wes Fox, at Marine Corps Command and Staff College. When presented with any challenge, he always encouraged us to ask the following questions: Is this our issue? Do we have the action on this one, or does it belong to another unit? Why are we having this headache? Remember lads, I would rather give a headache than have one. To be sure, Colonel Fox was a problem solver. He never backed away from any challenge, in or out of combat. He won the Medal of Honor during the Viet Nam War leading his decimated company during Operation Dewey Canyon. He was quiet and humble, but when he spoke in his slow Virginian drawl, everyone listened. Colonel Fox was a reasoned man who sought to define the parameters of the challenge before trying to tackle it. He always reminded us to "stay in our own lane."

There is a lot we cannot control in our lives. If we have to make a decision, we should first and foremost get the facts. Never rush to judgment. Things are not always as they seem, especially when raising children. Parents need to stay in their lane if their kids are going to learn to handle life's decisions.

A case in point was my father's "light touch" when it came to counseling me and my siblings. He never told us the answers; he let us figure things out for ourselves. He ensured we looked at all sides of an issue before making our decisions. Most importantly, he let you fail. A case in point was when I quit high school for three days in 1965. I was having all those teenage issues with self-image, figuring out who I was and all those teen nightmares we all remember. I was doing ok in school, but I decided one day to just quit mid-way through eleventh grade.

My mom panicked and started to get real weepy, accusing me of only thinking about myself. "How can you be so selfish, Michael? Don't you understand what this will do to your future?" I loved Mom, but my mind was made up. I was going to drop out of school and work as a bagger at the base commissary. We waited for my dad to come home from work to tell him about my not-so-great plan.

When I told my dad about my decision, he was flat line and showed no emotion. He asked me if I had thought it through, especially the part about losing out on my education. He let me quit. He told me that he was upset with my decision, but he had confidence that I would figure things out. I worked bagging groceries for three days. My wages were my tips and I think I made about twenty bucks total. Defeated, I told my parents I wanted to go back to school.

My dad showed great wisdom in letting me make my own decision. He could have demanded that I stay in school. But, he let me fail. Sometimes the only way to learn is to fail.

In the Marines, we always "wargamed" our decisions. Whenever we faced a tough issue or challenge, we always viewed it from three angles. What action should we take, what will the reaction be from our adversary, and finally, what should our counteraction be. This method of decision-making makes you look at the issue from a three-dimensional approach; today, tomorrow, and the day after tomorrow.

Life is a wargame. We make decisions and hope everything works out. We expect success. But we need a backup plan if things go wrong. To live your life any other way is setting yourself up for failure. Take the time to think things out. Ask others for their views and if you are the leader, get buy-in from your people. People support a plan they help develop, and don't fall in love with your plan! Be flexible and compromise. Don't be the oak tree that breaks apart in the stiff wind; be the willow tree that bends and lives on.

Always take ownership of your decisions. I know lots of people who back away from their decision if things go wrong. They look to blame others for the wrong turn on the road they turned on to. Try filtering all your decisions through the following lens, "Would this decision make my mom and dad proud of me?" Whether you are six or sixty, the answer to this simple question helps you stay moving in a positive direction on the road of life.

Rule 15: Stay Cool in Crisis

My earliest recollection of my dad's unflappable character was in 1955 when at six years of age I almost cut my finger off in a door jab. "John, come quick. Michael cut his finger really bad in the door." Dad said, "Mary, get a towel from the kitchen and wrap it up. Stop the bleeding and get him in the car now!" We drove to the Naval Air Station at Niagara Falls. No doctors were available; it was a weekend.

The ride in the car was chaotic, with my mom trying to stem the flow of blood with a bloody towel. My dad just looked straight ahead, like he was on a mission in his jet. I was really scared and in pain. The Navy corpsman said the finger might have to come off. My dad told him, "Just sew it back on."

The next thing I knew I was getting a shot and then I saw the needle and thread that were going to be used to stitch the tip of my finger back on. I was crying and so was my mom. Finally, Dad told Mom to leave the room and wait in the hallway. Dad never took his eyes off the stitching. As a father, I know he was really upset inside. But Dad did not show his emotions. He was cool under pressure.

My finger got sewed back on; fifteen or so stitches Mom told me. Up until the accident, I wrote with my right hand in school. Now, my finger was bandaged up so bad that I had to learn to write with my left hand.

Years later when Matt was in eighth grade, my bloody finger experience came back to me.

Matt and I were surfing one afternoon at Carlsbad Beach when Matt yelled from the shoreline, "Dad, I'm cut bad on my leg." His left leg was a bloody mess, and I thought he had been bit by a shark. I raced to him and immediately applied pressure to the wound. The lifeguards came and assisted with bandaging Matt's leg. I got him into our car and headed towards the hospital. I remembered Dad's expression and coolness under pressure as I made the drive. I tried to reassure him that it would be ok, just like my dad did with me back in 1955. I got him to the Camp Pendleton Hospital emergency room where he received twelve stitches in his leg. The wound was deep and only a few centimeters from his femoral artery.

Dana showed up when he was in the emergency room. Saying she was pissed off would be an understatement. Dana was upset because he would miss soccer practice. "What happened, Mike? This surfing has to go." Dana viewed surfing as a waste of time, which could have an adverse impact on Matt's soccer future. That said, Matt's surfing led to a career in lifeguarding.

Another example of cool under pressure involves my dear friend, Rich Higgins, and Captain Peter McCarthy. Peter was an Australian soldier who I served with in war-torn Lebanon in 1988. He had a wife and three children. One day on patrol, his jeep struck a roadside bomb and he was instantly killed. Our Observer Group mourned the loss of Peter, but we all knew we needed to get back on patrol. The exceptional leadership of our commander, Lt Col Rich Higgins USMC, focused all of us on our continuing mission to keep the peace in South Lebanon. He gathered all the officers together and made the following remarks:

> "I ask each of you to take a knee as we remember Peter. He was an exceptional husband, father, soldier, and friend. If he were here today, he would tell all of us to remember him in our prayers and help out his lovely wife and their children. The loss of life is tragic. Those of us who have been in combat know the face of death and the horror of war. It is an ugly thing. But it is not the ugliest of things. The ugliest thing is a man or woman who is not prepared, nor willing, to defend their freedoms and beliefs. Peter McCarthy paid the full measure defending the people of Lebanon from terrorists. He was a man of substance. He made a difference to all of us who knew him. May his soul rest in peace."

Rich then immediately pivoted and got everyone back to work. He knew from experience that the worst thing our unit could do would be to shut down and not get back to work. He knew that indecision and fear could jeopardize the mission and that we all needed to refocus on protecting the people of south Lebanon. Rich Higgins' exceptional leadership and character shown brightly in our moment of crisis.

Rule 16: Be Honest with Yourself and Others

Pride blocks our view of the truth. We get wrapped up in our own version of reality and can even convince ourselves that wrong is right. We call it rationalizing. We know we messed up, but we look for anything to justify our behaviors. "Everyone is doing it" becomes our motto.

When I was in sixth grade, we had a lot of adventures in the canyon around the corner from our house. We built grass huts and explored caves. We would leave the house in the early morning and get back just before the sun set. Mom and Dad did not worry about me and my sister, Joan. I looked out for Joanie.

One day a friend of mine, Ronnie, brought some matches with him to our grass hut. We were sitting in the hut and he thought it would be a good idea to build a fire on the grass hut's dirt floor. I knew that it was a horrible idea and told him I was going home. I took my sister with me and we walked back to our house.

About thirty minutes later, we heard the fire engines. The field was on fire. It took the fire department about thirty minutes to put out the flames. I did not tell my mom and dad about the matches and that Ronnie had probably started the fire.

The next morning, the police came to our house. One officer said that someone had reported that it was me who had started the fire. I knew right then and there that Ronnie's parents had blamed me for the fire. I told the policeman what had happened. "I will go back and see Ronnie's parents and get this straightened out. The fine for starting a fire is over 1000 dollars," he said. One thousand dollars was a ton of money!

My dad was very upset with me and said, *"Bad news does not get better with time. You should have immediately told me what happened yesterday, Mike. The fire may have been prevented."* I felt really bad because I knew that I had let my dad down.

Ronnie did finally admit he started the fire and his parents were fined. I learned a lot from the fire incident. Ronnie was not my friend. He lied about me and no friend does that. Friends are always honest and have each other's backs. Make sure you choose your friends wisely in this life and remember the cover-up is worse than the lie. "'Tis a tangled web we weave, when we first practice to deceive." Dad said this a lot.

Telling the truth is always the best policy, but it can have bad consequences. Matt Sullivan, unlike Ronnie, learned to tell the truth at an early age. Matt always followed John around and looked up to him as his big brother. I could always read Matt like a book. He wore his emotions on his sleeves. John, on the other hand, was a little more guarded in his feelings. I could always tell when Matt was covering for John, and I would call him out for it. I never doubted any of my kids' honesty, but Matt was always intensely honest. Let me give you an example.

When Matt graduated from high school, he went to work as a lifeguard for Camp Pendleton. He had the ideal job. When he was not working or taking a surf trip, he partied with the boys. On one occasion, his crew was drinking at a state beach when a lifeguard approached them and asked, "Who does the beer can on the fence belong to?" Matt responded, "It is my can." The guard asked for his ID card. When they saw his age, eighteen, they issued him a citation. The story gets better.

Matt had to go to court for the ticket. He told me later he expected a fine. The judge suspended his license for six months. Without a license, he could not work as a lifeguard. He finally told me about the ticket when he got back from court. I was upset that he did not give me a heads up before he went to court. Now, we were in damage control. Matt said that the beer can was his. He did not want to see any of his friends get burned. He did what comes naturally to him. He told the truth.

Fortunately, Kerrie's softball pitching coach was a lawyer who was very well connected. Good timing! I talked to him and asked for his help. The next day, he got Matt back in front of the judge who restored his privilege to drive to, during, and from work. Saved by the bell! Matt survived and is still lifeguarding today.

When it comes to honesty, it takes courage to face the truth. I'm reminded of one of my childhood baseball heroes,

Mickey Mantle. He was an eighteen-year-old Oklahoma kid who was recruited in 1952 to be the New York Yankees' center fielder. Mickey had a record second to none in both fielding and in hitting. He led the Yankees to five World Series Championships and won multiple batting crowns. As a young Little Leaguer, all I wanted was to wear number seven on my uniform: Mickey's number. Mickey and another Yankee, Roger Maris, were both going after Babe Ruth's home run record in 1961. Maris hit 61 home runs and Mickey was right behind him with 59. To an eleven-year-old boy, Mickey Mantle could do no wrong. He was invincible.

However, his bouts of heavy drinking were legendary. After retiring from baseball, he had several failed businesses and finally ended up signing autographs in shopping malls. He lost his family. His wife, Meryl, and three of his four sons were treated for alcoholism. Mickey lost two sons before he passed.

Mickey went through alcohol rehabilitation and converted to Christianity before he died of liver cancer in 1990. He made a video before he died. He ended the video by saying, "I was a role model; don't end up like me." Mickey died a lonely death. To me, Mickey's finest hour was when he had the courage to admit defeat and be truthful with all his fans. He could not self-medicate his way out of his problems. The party ends for all of us; hopefully, we still have our family at our side when we bow out.

Being honest with yourself can be painful. As with any addiction, recovery starts when you admit you have a problem. In 1988, I admitted I had an alcohol problem. I was not a social drinker; I often lost control when I drank. While I was going through alcohol rehab, I remembered what Grandpa John had said about the "Irish curse." I remembered the part about his father deserting the family for a woman and "drink." I did not want to lose my family and I have not had a drink in thirty-two years.

It can be difficult to navigate in a fog, but with patience, you get to your destination. You have to slow down and depend on your headlights. In life, we often get into situations where we don't know which way to turn. A Marine friend of mine said, "Sully, these things always work out. Stay the course." He was right. The truth eventually surfaces. What looks like a mountain turns out to be a hill. Like a light, truth guides us through the most difficult times of our lives.

Rule 17: Have Faith

Faith evolves. Sometimes you lose it. If you are lucky, you will rediscover God and get back on track. If you try to fix things yourself without God's help, you will eventually fail. Believing in your higher power is the only way to survive when life crushes you.

We need to play the long game in life. Our lives are not measured in seconds, hours, or even years. Rather, our lives are measured by the totality of our contributions to others. Life is a marathon, not a sprint. It is not how fast you run the laps; it is staying in the race that counts. We must endure the good times and the bad times.

Everyone gets knocked down in life. How we handle our failures and disappointments is the true measure of our character. If we have faith, we can get through any challenge. We all suffer. How we handle defeat and personal setbacks determines our character.

When I was a child, going to church seemed like a chore. It took me away from my friends. You have to sit quietly and listen to some priest or minister say a lot of stuff you really do not understand. Once in a while, the priest would say something that I connected to, like the talk about the devil, sin, and damnation. That stuff scared me then and it still does.

Dad always said, "Going to church is like having an insurance policy." He believed that death was just around the corner, so we all better be ready for it if it came your way. Having been through two wars and seeing a lot of death gave him a different perspective on life than the rest of us in the family.

Dad always referred to priests as "men of the cloth," which is an old Irish saying. I remember one of our parish priests, Father Joseph Stadler.

Our church caught on fire one Saturday night in 1959. He entered the burning building and rescued the tabernacle where the communion hosts were being kept for Sunday's masses. He had already blessed the hosts Saturday afternoon and they had become the body of Christ (Catholic belief). He retrieved the tabernacle, but not before his hands were severely burned. The story of Father Stadler saving the hosts is one that I will always remember. He was an inspiration to the entire parish.

I remember my first Holy Communion, as well as all the Saturday morning classes to prepare us for the sacrament. The Nuns taught us our catechism lessons. Going to confession the first time was a little overwhelming for an eight-year-old boy. I remember how serious it all seemed.

Sixty years after my first communion, a lot has happened to me. I got married, retired from the Marine Corps, parented three children with Dana, and suffered the loss of my son. Both my parents are gone. But my faith endures.

Dana and I raised our kids in the Catholic faith. We always went to church on Sunday and both boys became altar boys. I fell away from regular church attendance around 1996. I got lazy. I convinced myself that my faith was a "personal thing." The Pacific Ocean became my new church and my sons and I all surfed every weekend. Dana and I did not attend church with any of the kids. We just fell away like many other Catholic families. I figured we were all leading good lives and that we were all just fine with the Lord. We had been spared from any real family tragedy. John's death caught us all off guard.

I think you have to believe in God in a childlike fashion if you are going to be a person of faith. If you try to analyze God's existence, or figure out why the world is broke, you will get nowhere. The sooner you come to the conclusion that the world is filled with chaos and tragedy, the better you appreciate the good things you have been given in this life. I have found the less I worry and just let things go, the better I can cope with the ups and downs of life. This approach to life is easy to say, but really hard to put into practice. There is an old saying, "Let go, let God." These are good words to live by.

Really bad things happen to good people and there is little you can do to change reality. Sometimes things really do happen for a reason. When failure occurs, we always try to figure out what we could have done differently. Some of us obsess over failure and never recover.

When John died, I made it my mission to take care of his kids, Ayden and Ava. Dana and I continue to love and support the kids. About three years ago, I felt the need to go inside the Catholic church located just down the street from where I live. I had never been inside the new church. As I entered the front door, our Irish parish priest was exiting. We locked eyeballs and he said, "You look troubled. Can I help?"

We talked for about ten minutes. He told me not to worry so much about John's soul and to come back to Mass on Sunday. Divine providence? I believe so. I am practicing my faith today.

You cannot just sit on the bench in life, you have to get into the game. But we are just the players and God makes the rules. We can fight it, or accept it. Most of us want to be in control of our lives. We figure that if we do good, good will come our way. When that curveball comes at us, we either stay in the batter's box or bail out. Most of my life, I like to think I stayed in the box and took a swing. I try to remember that each day is a gift. Each day we have the opportunity to make the world a little brighter for those around us. Most importantly, each day we will be challenged and our character will be tested.

So, that's it. As Forrest Gump would say, "That's all I have to say about that." You can learn a lot by watching the Tom Hanks character in the movie, "Forrest Gump." Forrest is humble, respectful, patient, loyal, hard-working, and always overcomes his challenges. Despite his mental limitations, he becomes a high school football hero, Medal of Honor winner, world-renowned ping pong champ, long-distance runner, husband, father, and above all—a devoted son.

If the world were filled with people like Forrest, it would be a better place.

We all have an impact on each other. What we say and do can make or break another human being. One man or woman can make a difference. A kind word or two from us can make someone's day. If we mess something up, no problem. Take ownership of your mistakes and apologize. I seldom hear the words, "I'm sorry." People are quick to blame others. No one listens. God gave us two ears and one mouth. If we listened twice as much as we talked, we might actually appreciate the other person's point of view.

Of this I am sure: the simple rules in this book work. We complicate life with a lot of meaningless material stuff. In fact, we only take two things out of this world: faith and love. The faith comes from believing in your higher power and staying on the field until we are called home. The love comes from what we give others and the love that is given to us in return. It is that simple.

Author Bio

Mike is a decorated retired career Marine officer and educator. A California native, he spent most of his military service serving multiple tours at Camp Pendleton where he and his wife, Dana, raised their three children. As a Marine officer, he commanded units from the platoon level through the battalion level. Upon retiring from the Marines, he taught high school and served as a faculty development coordinator for the Marine Corps Command and Staff College. The son of a career naval officer, Mike's upbringing had a significant impact on his character development and faith. Husband, father, and grandfather, Mike's life has been filled with challenges and significant hurdles. His life lessons are applicable to young and old alike. Boiling life down to the essential rules of the road, Sullivan Strong is a blueprint for overcoming fear and disappointment and achieving happiness in our chaotic world.